JOHN ADAMS
SHORT RIDE IN A FAST MACHINE

FOR 1 PIANO, 4 HANDS

HENDON MUSIC

DISTRIBUTED BY

7777 W. BLUEMOUND RD. P.O. BOX 13819 MILWAUKEE, WI 53213

www.boosey.com
www.halleonard.com

The idea for this arrangement arose in Miami, FL, during a visit we had with John Adams at the New World Symphony in 2016. Over coffee, conversation turned to some of his orchestral works, and John suddenly observed that his *Short Ride in a Fast Machine* could prove to be a very interesting four-hand piano work. We hesitated for about one strike of a woodblock before responding "Yes!!!!" So with the expert engagement of John's student, Preben Antonsen, after a brief collaboration between the four of us, the four hand piano version of Short Ride in a Fast Machine was born.

In addition to being a brilliant adaptation of the orchestral piece, the four-hand version of Short Ride independently deserves a prominent place in the four-hand piano repertoire. Just as a black and white photo can capture beauty and detail not readily apparent in color, transcribing the spectacular orchestration to piano alone reveals additional rhythmic and tonal aspects of this masterpiece.

We hope you enjoy this piece. When we began performing the work we experienced with surprise that not only does it paint an aural picture of a Short Ride; when sitting side by side at the piano it feels as though every bone in our body is being taken on a "short ride in a fast machine" that is exhilarating for the performer and listener alike.

*Note for performers: The distribution as appears in the score is how we felt most comfortable... But feel free to designate notes between the two players in the way that feels right for you!

—Christina and Michelle Naughton

Recorded by Christina and Michelle Naughton
Warner Classics 190295562298

for Christina & Michelle Naughton

SHORT RIDE IN A FAST MACHINE

JOHN ADAMS
arr. Preben Antonsen

979-0-051-10813-8

Printed in USA
Printed in 2019

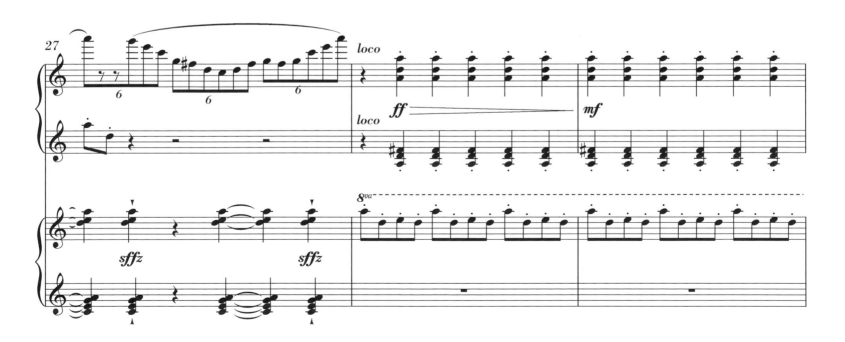

both hands 8va

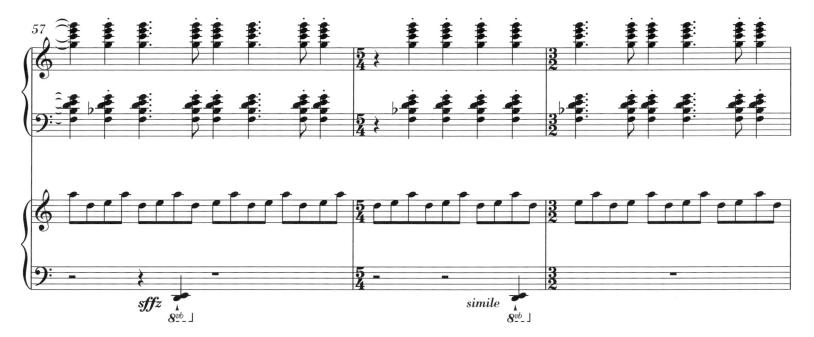

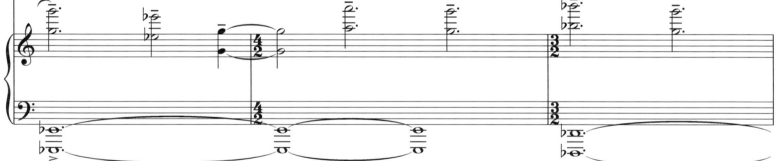

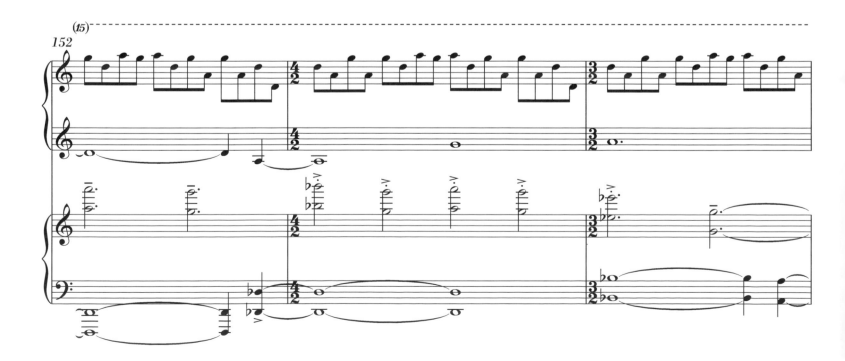

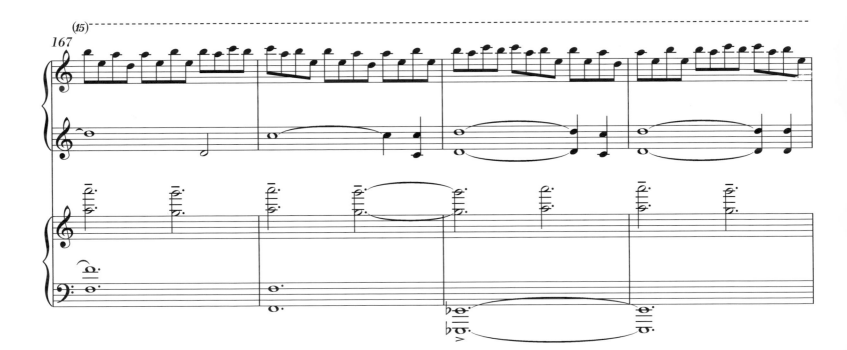

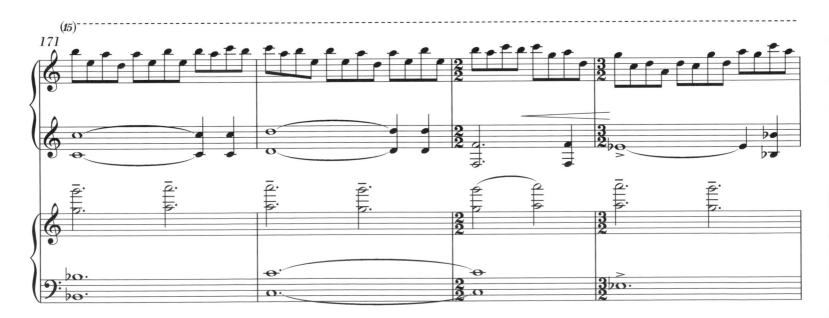

* Piano I's final two measures (from the original orchestral piece played by the Woodwinds)
  may be played and / or embellished based on the the harmony transcribed .